THE BIG DINO-PEDIA FOR SMALL LEARNERS

Dinosaur Books for Kids
Children's Animal Books

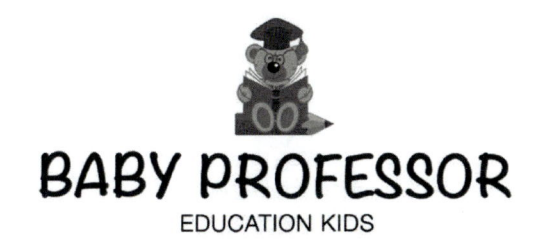

BABY PROFESSOR
EDUCATION KIDS

Speedy Publishing LLC
40 E. Main St. #1156
Newark, DE 19711
www.speedypublishing.com
Copyright 2017

All Rights reserved. No part of this book may be reproduced or used in any way or form or by any means whether electronic or mechanical, this means that you cannot record or photocopy any material ideas or tips that are provided in this book

Humans have been around for a long time, maybe as much as two million years. That sounds like a lot! But it really isn't all that long when you compare it to the dinosaurs. They ruled the earth for about 165 million years. They were around 80 times longer than humans have managed so far.

Here's a grab-bag of facts about dinosaurs: the biggest, the smallest, the meanest, and the mildest. Read on and become a dino-expert!

COOL DUDe

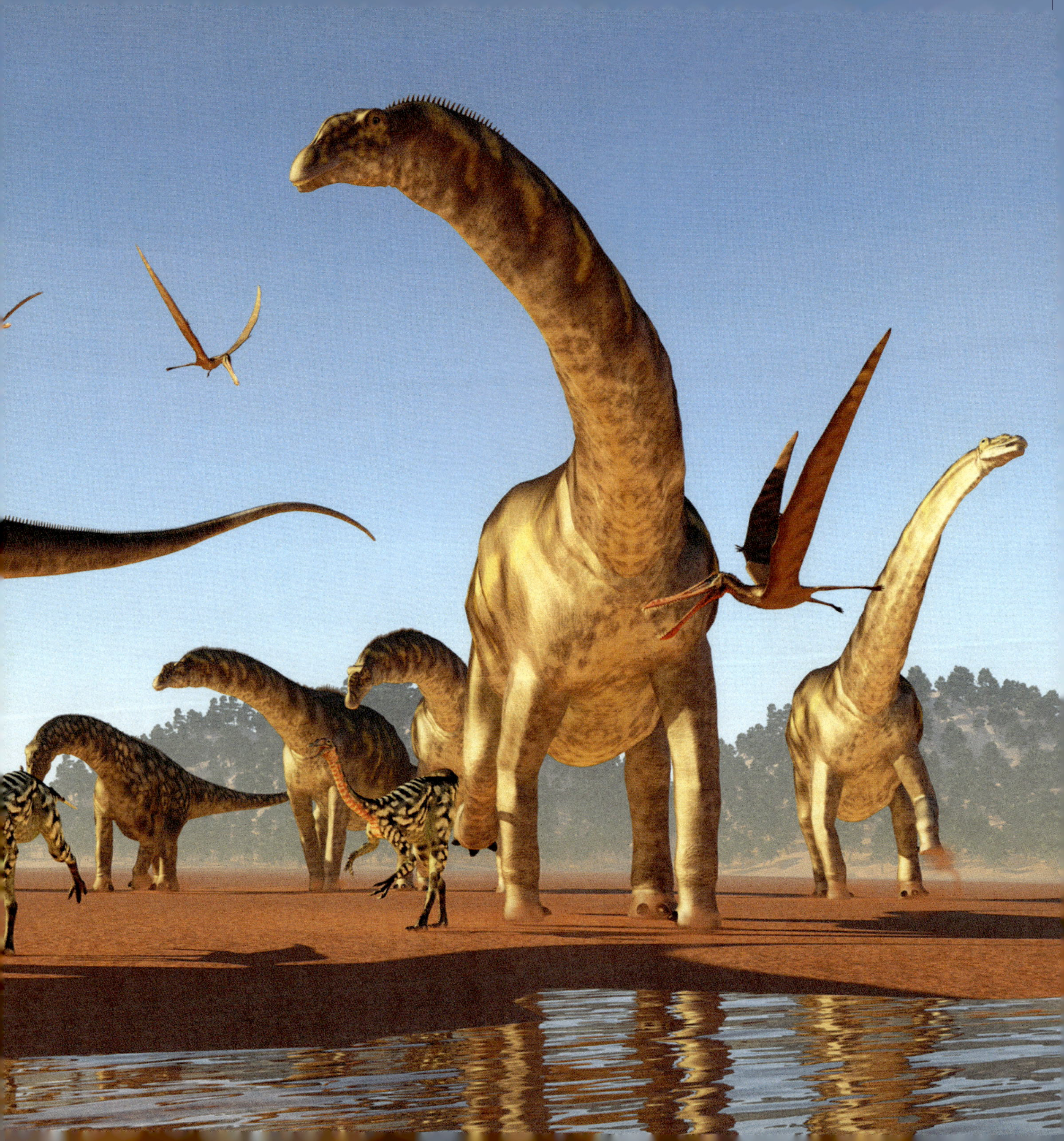

A WORLD OF DINOSAURS

Dinosaurs were reptiles. They are related to today's snakes, lizards, and, strangely enough, birds. They lived throughout the world, long before people existed.

When the dinosaurs lived, there were also animals that lived in the oceans, and there were flying lizards. But none of them were true dinosaurs. Dinosaurs were land animals.

Dinosaurs lived on every continent, including Antarctica. However, in the age of dinosaurs the continents we know today were all joined together in one large land mass, so it was much easier for dinosaurs to move around than it would be today.

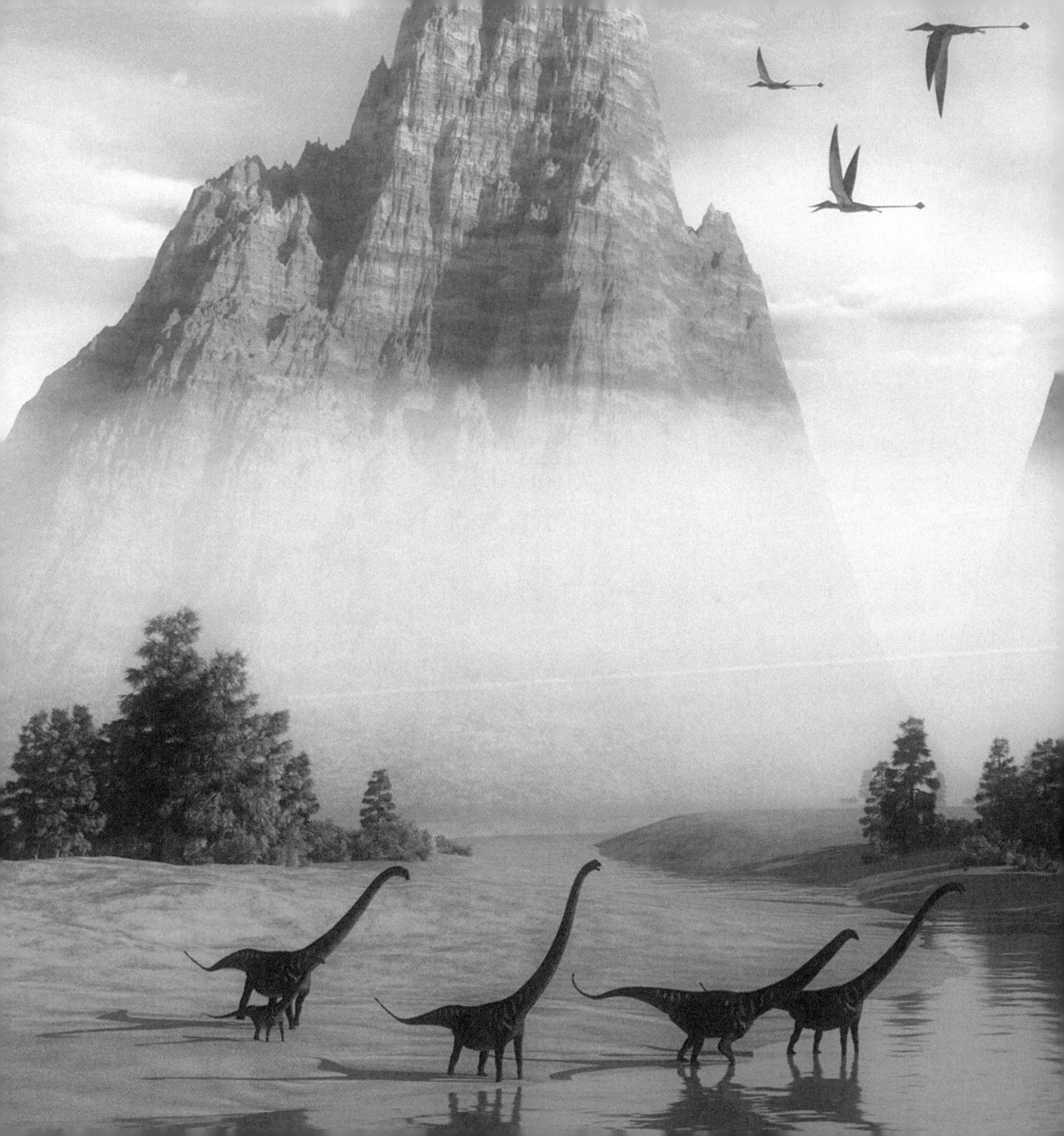

They did not have to swim to get where they wanted to go! In the millions of years since the time of the dinosaurs, the continents have moved apart into the map we now know.

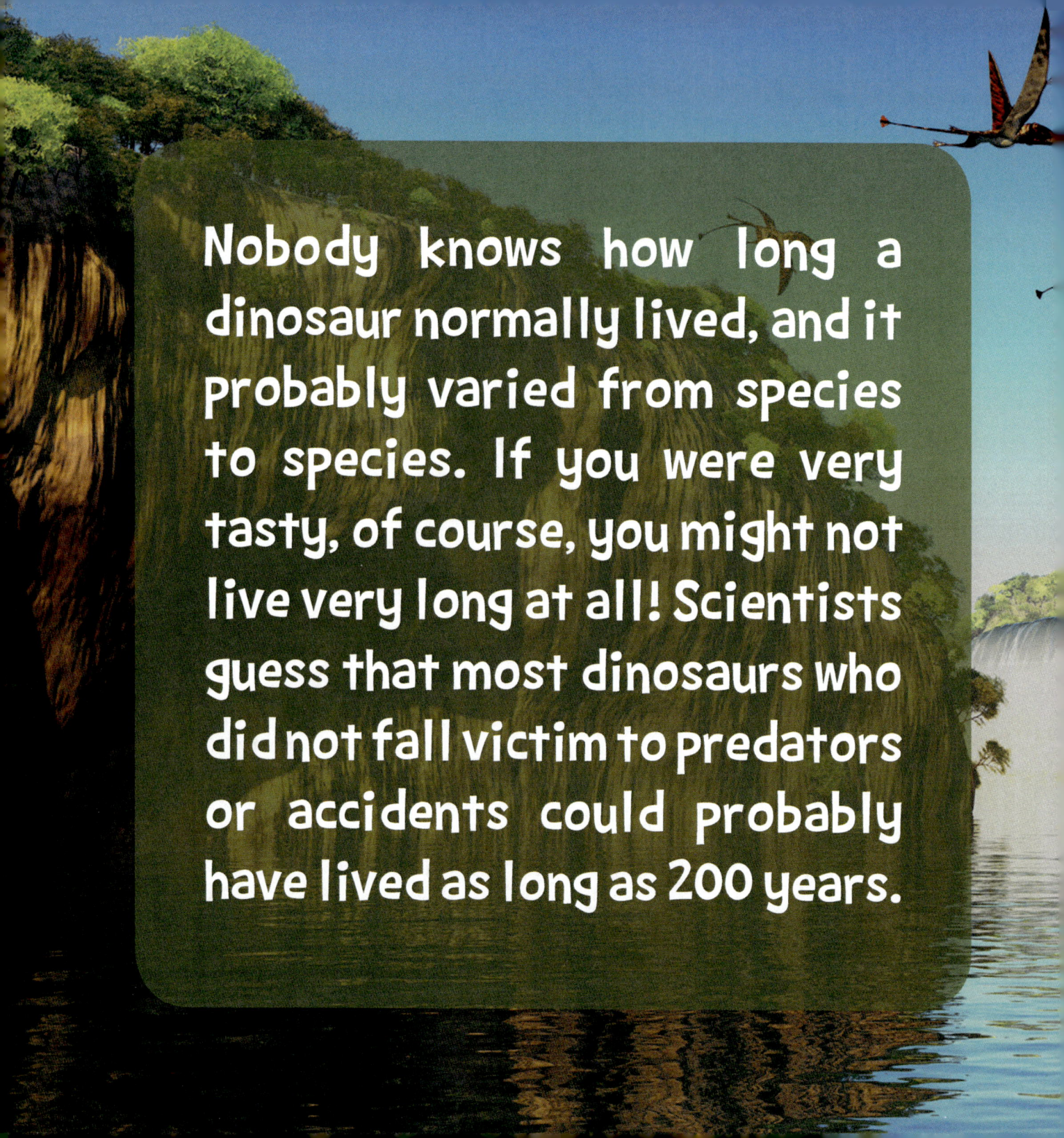

Nobody knows how long a dinosaur normally lived, and it probably varied from species to species. If you were very tasty, of course, you might not live very long at all! Scientists guess that most dinosaurs who did not fall victim to predators or accidents could probably have lived as long as 200 years.

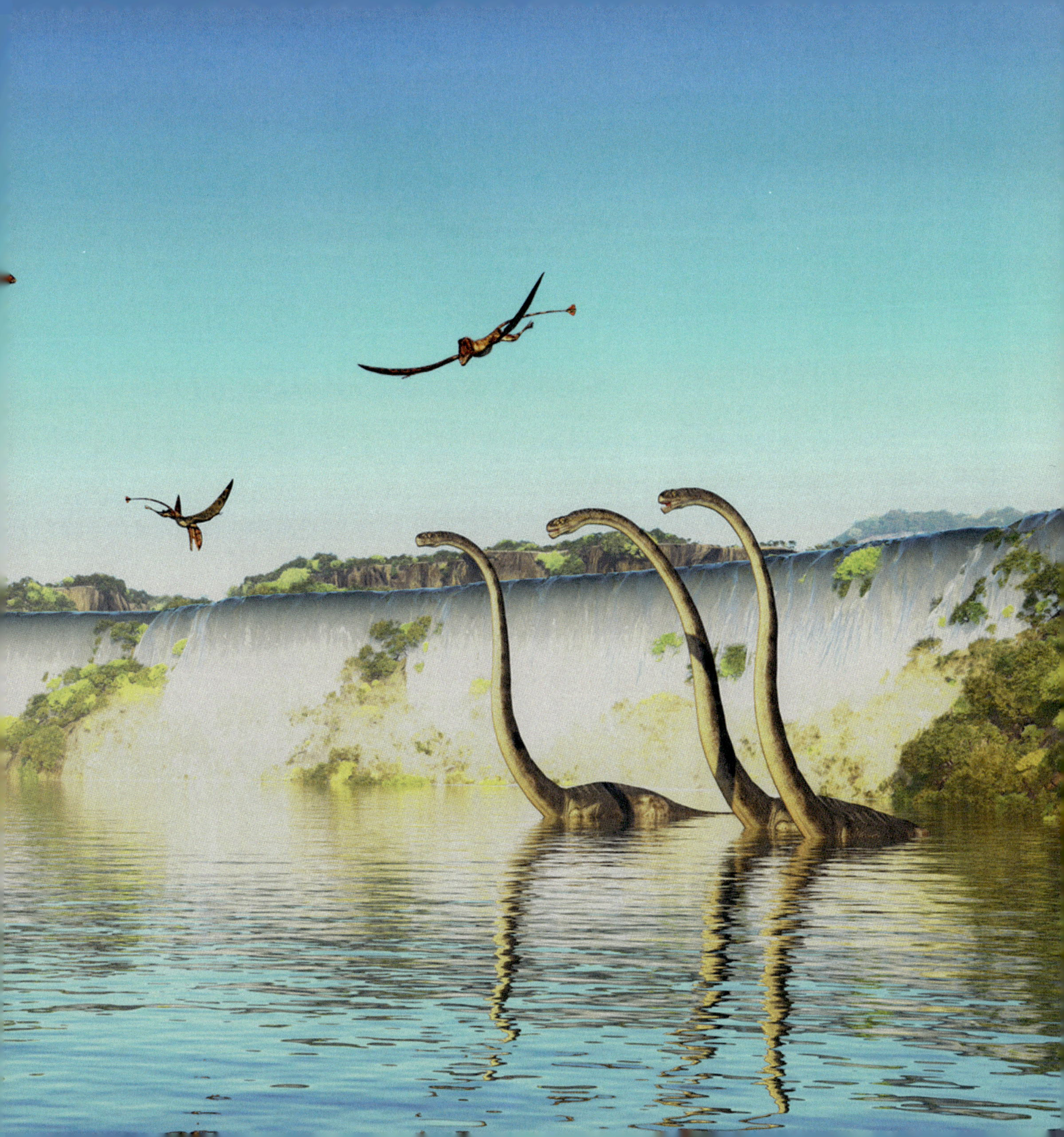

We think of dinosaurs as huge creatures, but most of them were more or less the size of humans or horses. Scientists think that the larger bones get preserved and fossilized better than the bones of smaller dinosaurs, and that's why we find more bones belonging to the larger species.

All dinosaurs laid eggs. Scientists have found 40 different types of dinosaur eggs so far. But there is no way to make these eggs hatch into dinosaurs because they have been fossilized (turned into rocks).

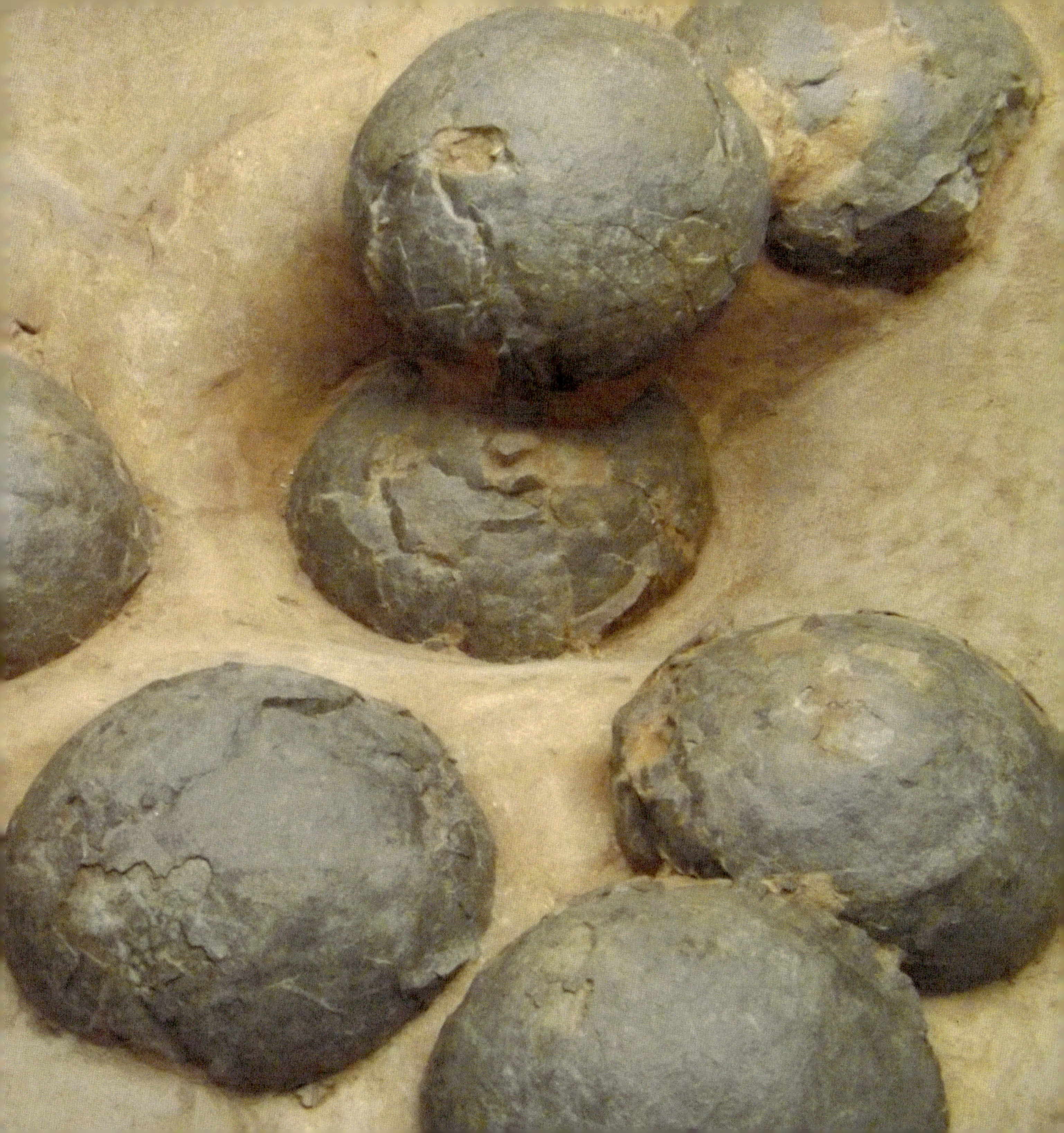

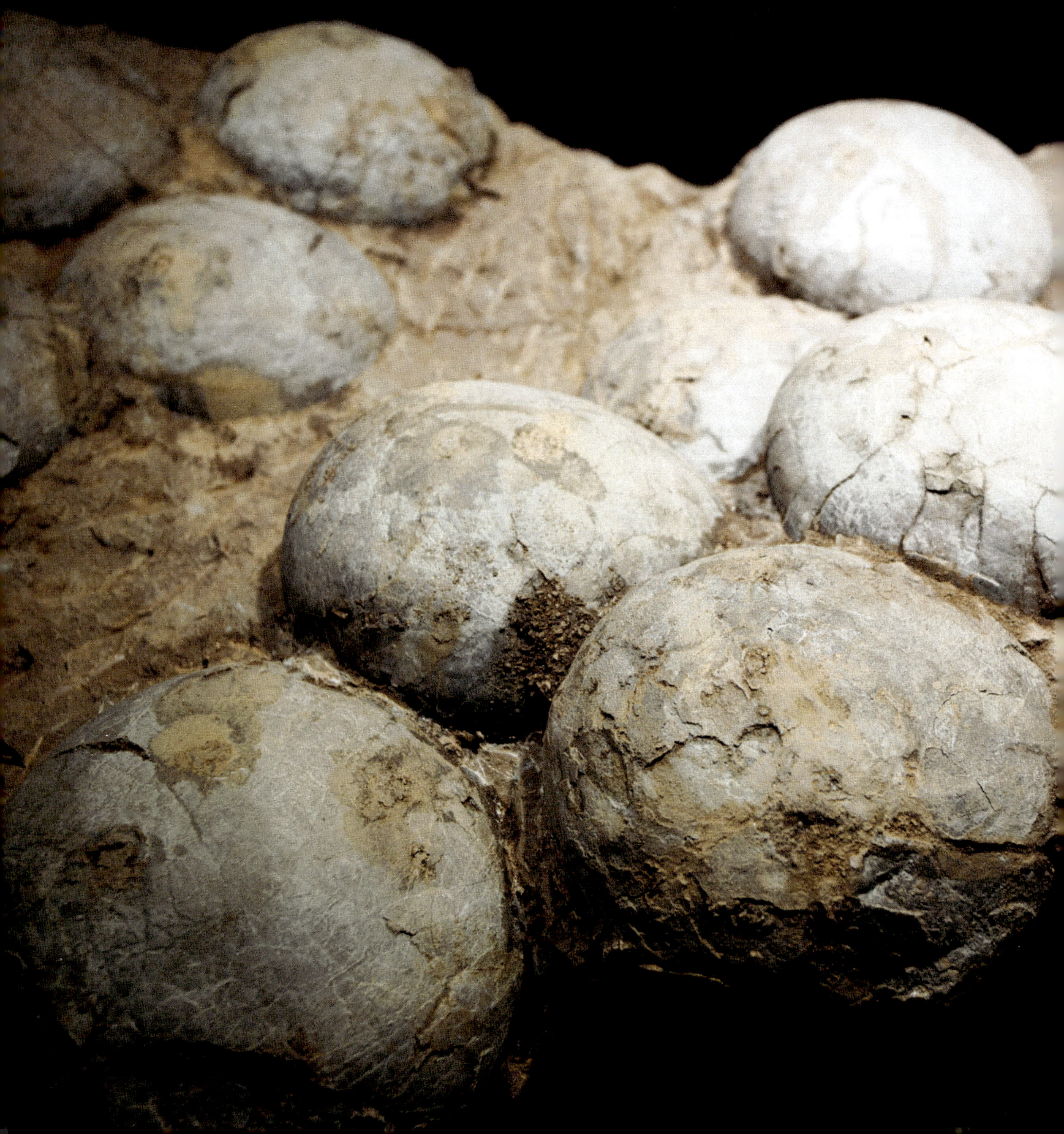

The largest dinosaur eggs we have found so far are about the size of basketballs. Dinosaurs built nests for their eggs, and may have protected the nest to keep the eggs safe and warm. Some species may have nurtured and fed their young until they were old enough to take care of themselves.

DIFFERENT TYPES OF DINOSAURS

At a very basic level, there were two types of dinosaurs. One type ate grasses and other plants, and the other type ate meat. Meat-eating dinosaurs are called "theropods", meaning that they usually had sharp claws on their toes that helped them kill their prey and slice up their bodies. Vegetarian dinosaurs had stumpier feet, like horse hooves or elephants' feet.

Large plant-eating dinosaurs had to eat as much as a school-bus worth of vegetation every day. It would be easy to find where they had been as they chewed their way through fields and forests! The plant-eating dinosaurs probably travelled in herds, the way modern plant-eating animals tend to do.

There is another way of grouping dinosaurs: by the structure of their hips. There are lizard-hipped (saurischian) dinosaurs and bird-hipped (ornithischian) dinosaurs. For lizard-hipped dinosaurs, one of the hip bones points backwards, as it does in modern lizards.

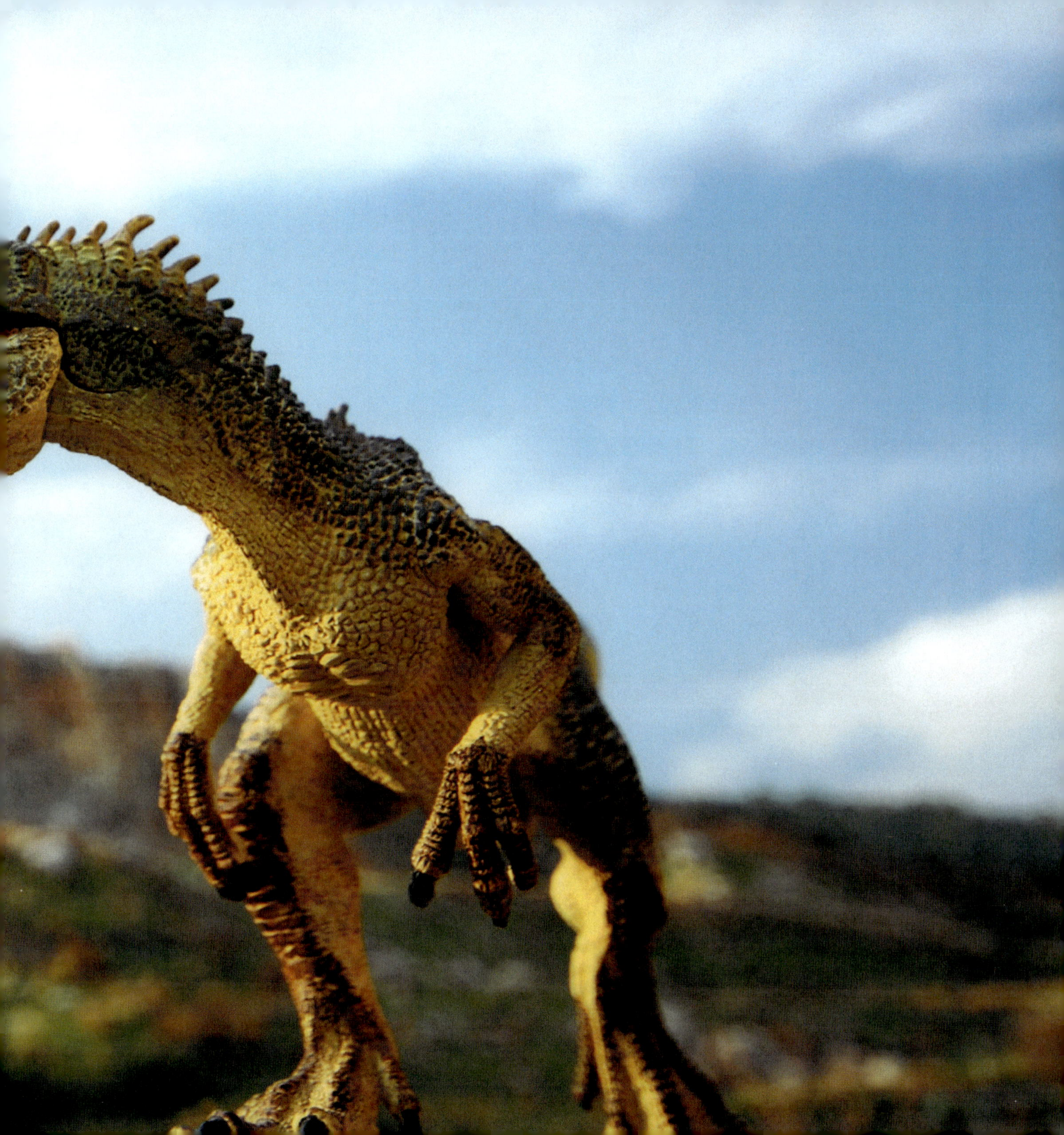

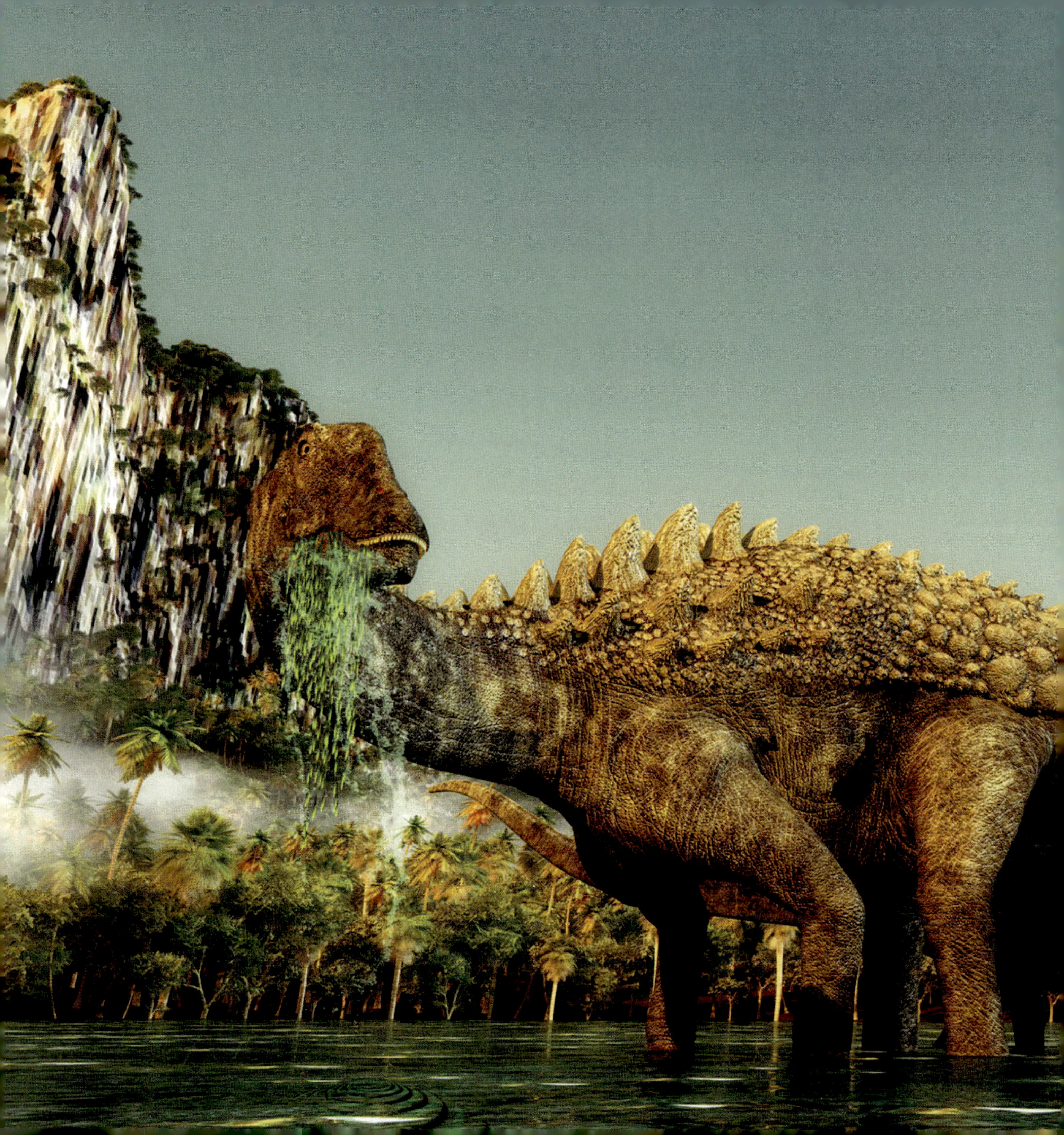

For the other type, all the hip bones point backwards, as they do for modern birds. The funny thing is, modern birds evolved from dinosaurs, but not from the bird-hipped ones. They seem to have evolved from lizard-hipped ancestors.

We know of at least 1000 different dinosaur types, but many more types might have existed. Every time we find new dinosaur remains, we discover things that people had not known before. For example, only recently have we discovered that many dinosaurs may not have been green like lizards, but might have had bright feathers all over their bodies!

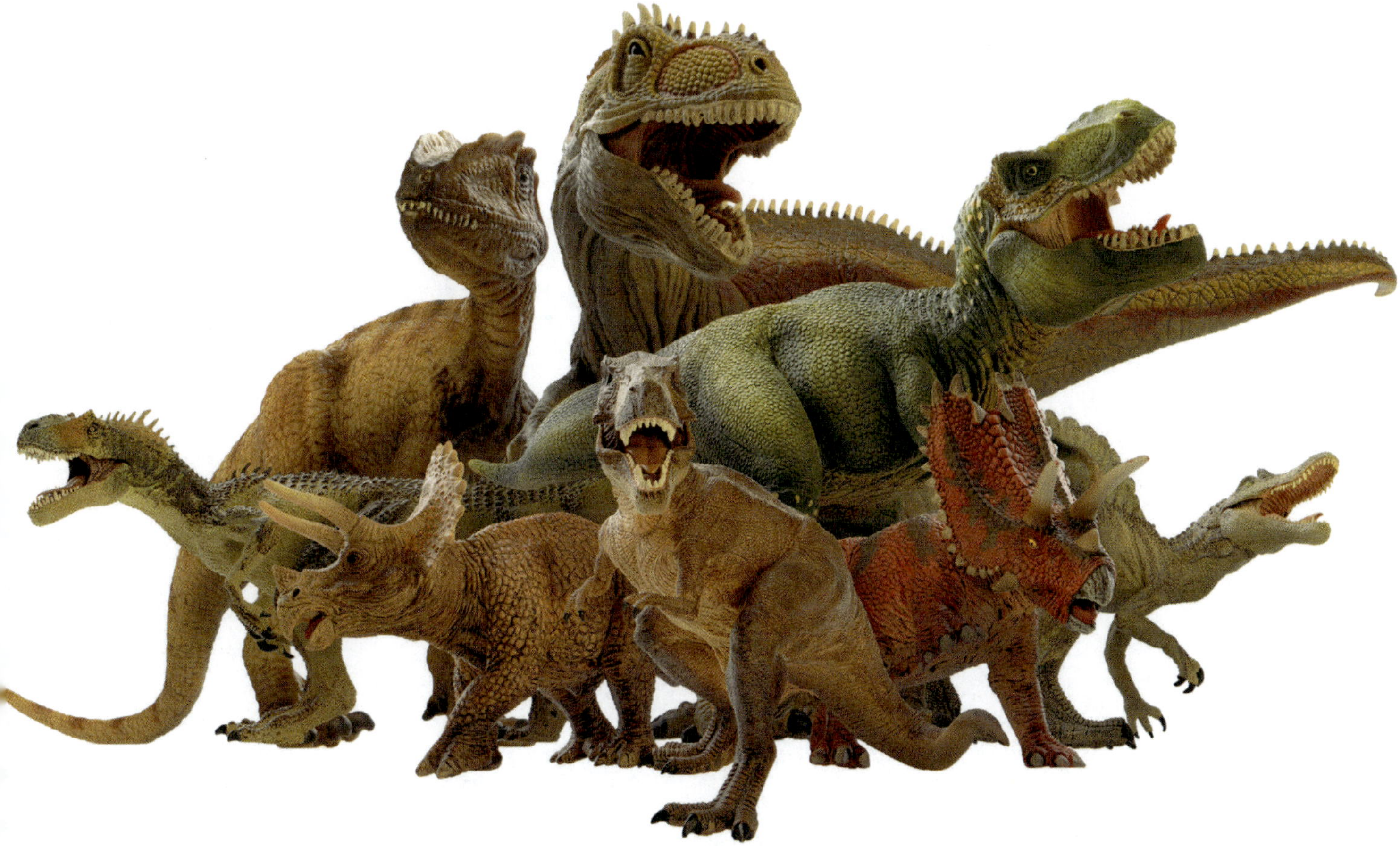

DINOSAUR BODIES

Touch your own head. Slide your fingers all around, and you will find that it feels pretty solid except for the holes for your mouth, nostrils, ears, and eyes. Dinosaur skulls were quite different. They had all the holes for their ears, eyes, and mouth, but they also had open places to make the skull lighter. Some dinosaur skulls would be as big as a car, so making them lighter would be important! The skin stretched over those open spaces so you would not see them from the outside, but they must have been easy to hurt the dinosaur through those places if another dinosaur attacked.

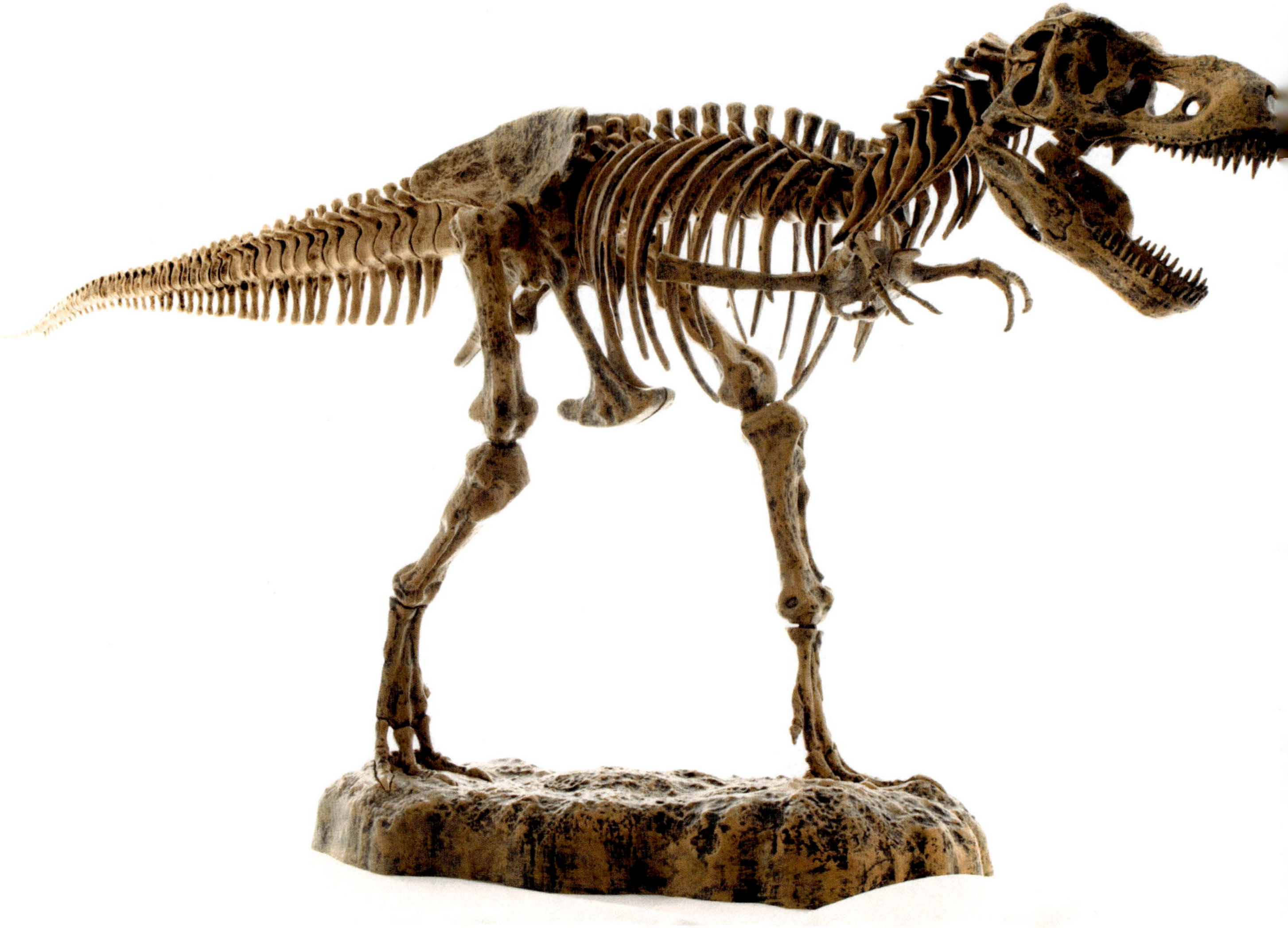

For the big dinosaurs, their bones could be huge. But some of the bones were lighter than you might think. The bones of the meat-eaters were hollow, like bird bones, so the dinosaur could move quickly and would not collapse under its own weight.

Some of the larger dinosaurs had tails that could be as much as 45 feet long. The long tails helped the dinosaurs keep their balance when they were moving or fighting. When you're that big, you really don't want to slip and fall down!

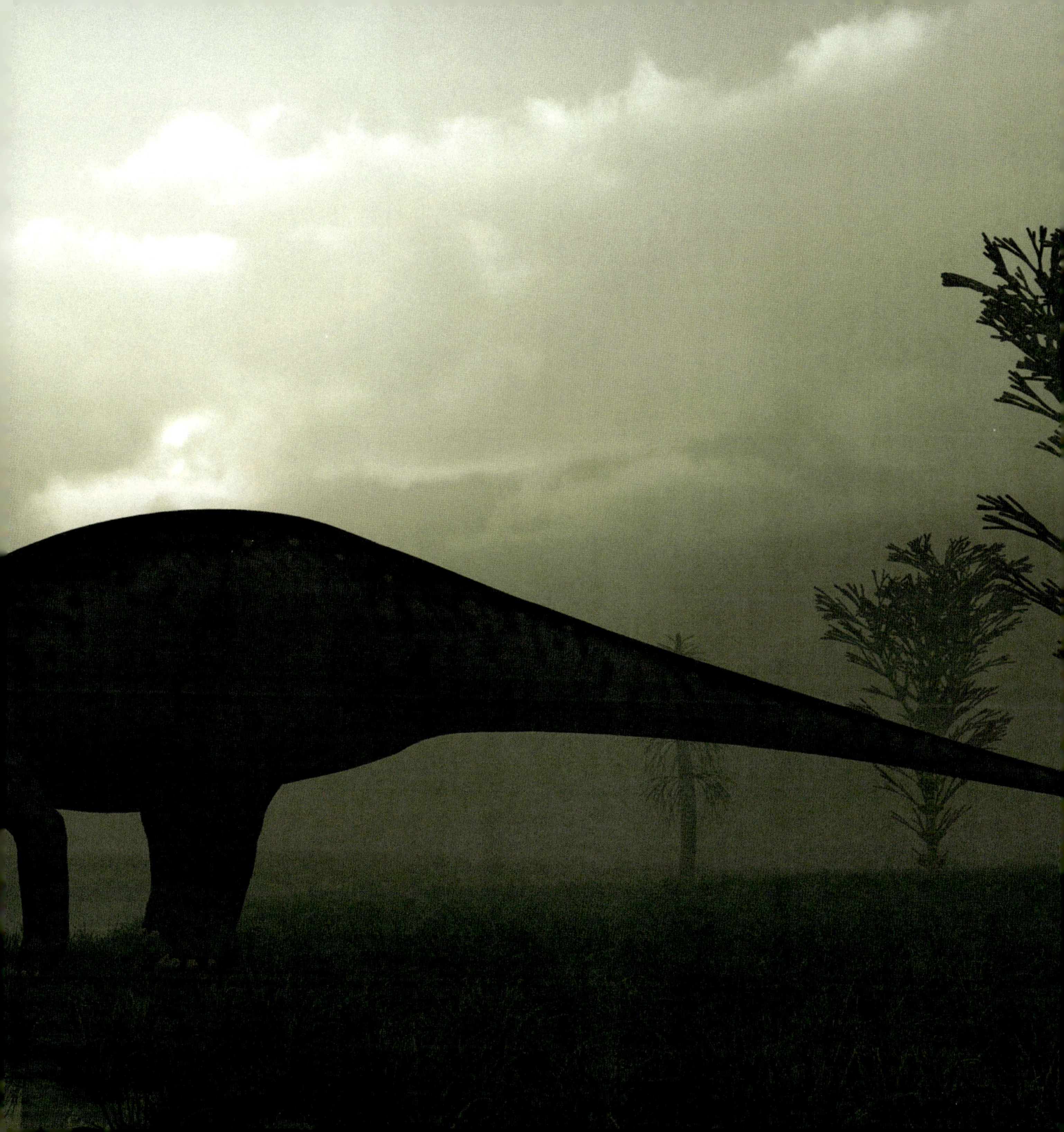

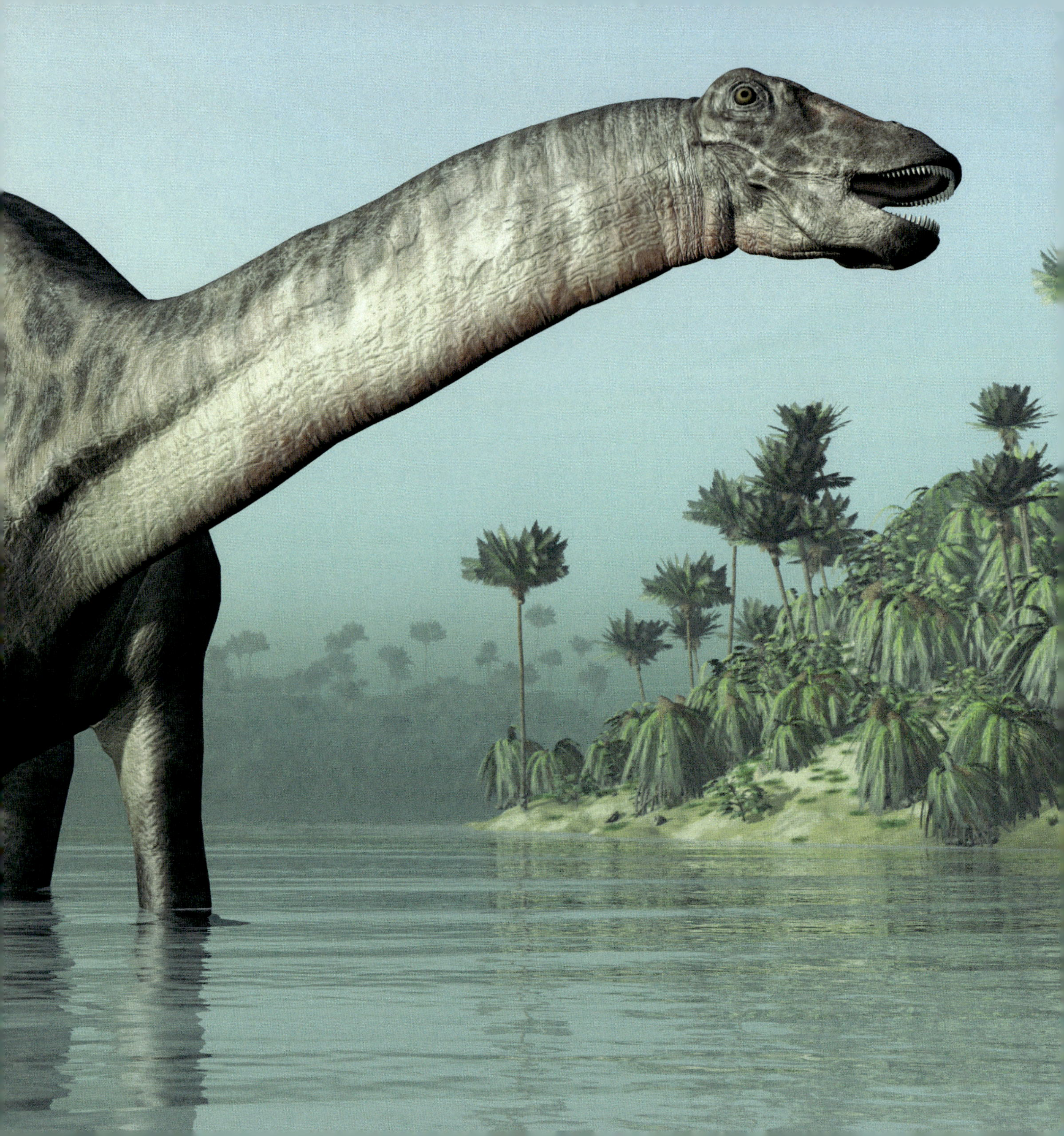

There were both cold-blooded dinosaurs, like today's lizards and snakes, and warm-blooded dinosaurs, like modern mammals. There may even have been dinosaurs who did not fit neatly into these two types. Warm-blooded dinosaurs were probably small meat-eaters, while most of the large plant-eaters were probably cold-blooded.

Plant-eating dinosaurs walked on all fours so they could hold up their large bodies, although some may have been able to stand on two legs while reaching up for branches of trees. Meat-eaters mostly travelled on two legs, which left their front legs free to help them attack and hold their prey.

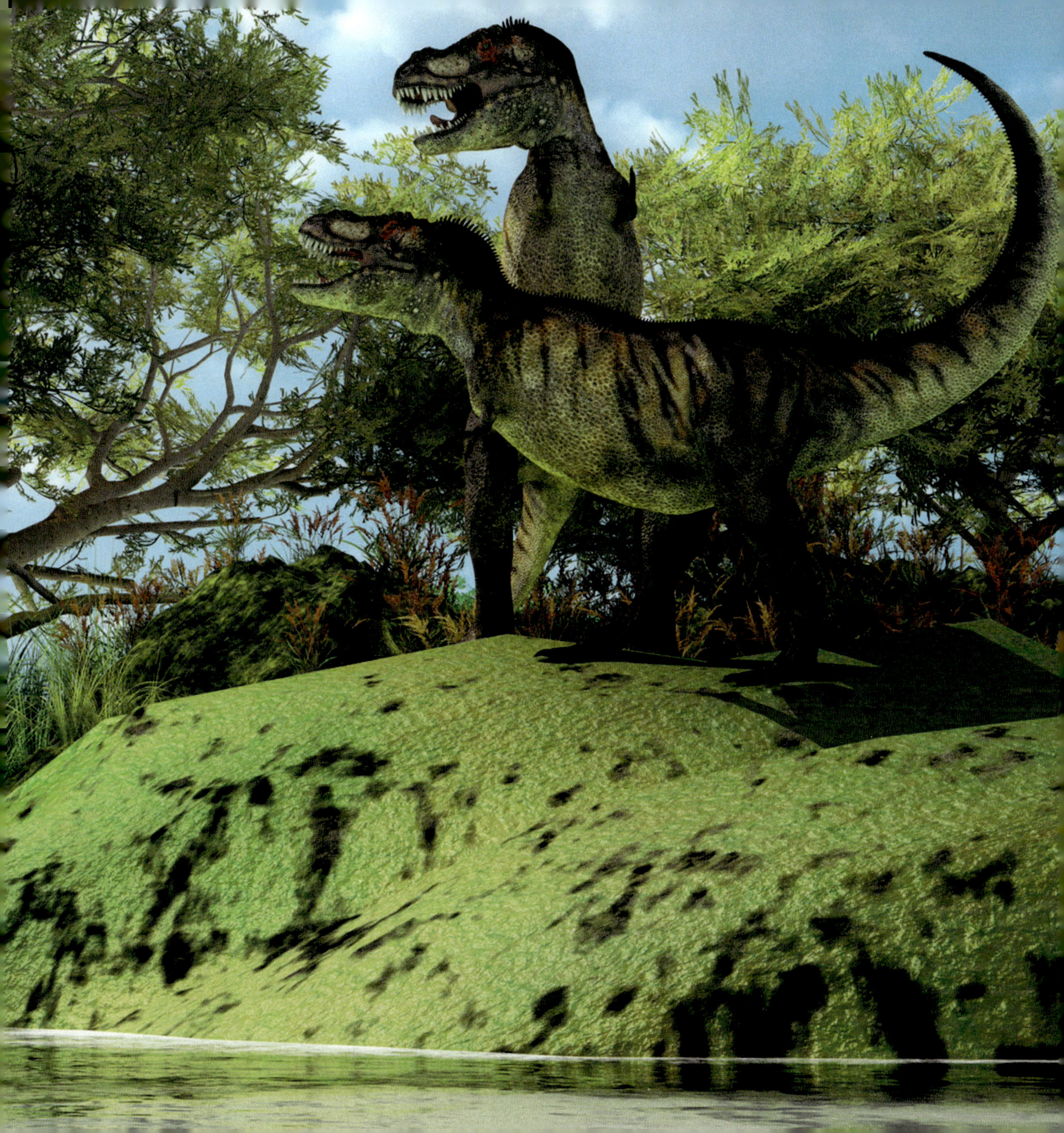

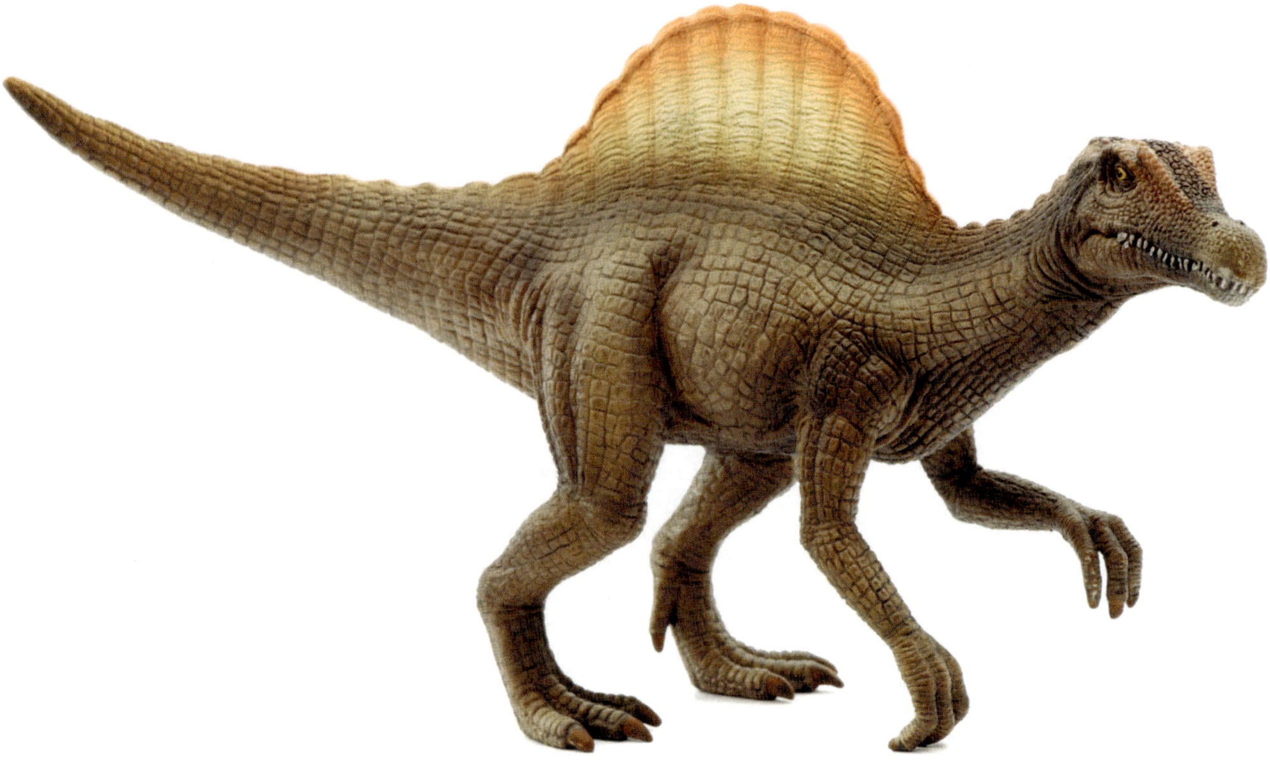

Dinosaurs did not have large brains. A large adult dinosaur had a smaller brain than a new-born human baby has. The Stegosaurus had a body as large as a small truck, but its brain was smaller than a golf ball. Small, meat-eating dinosaurs probably had the largest brains compared to their body size.

Modern lizards and snakes shed their skin as they outgrow it. Scientists think that some dinosaurs may have done the same.

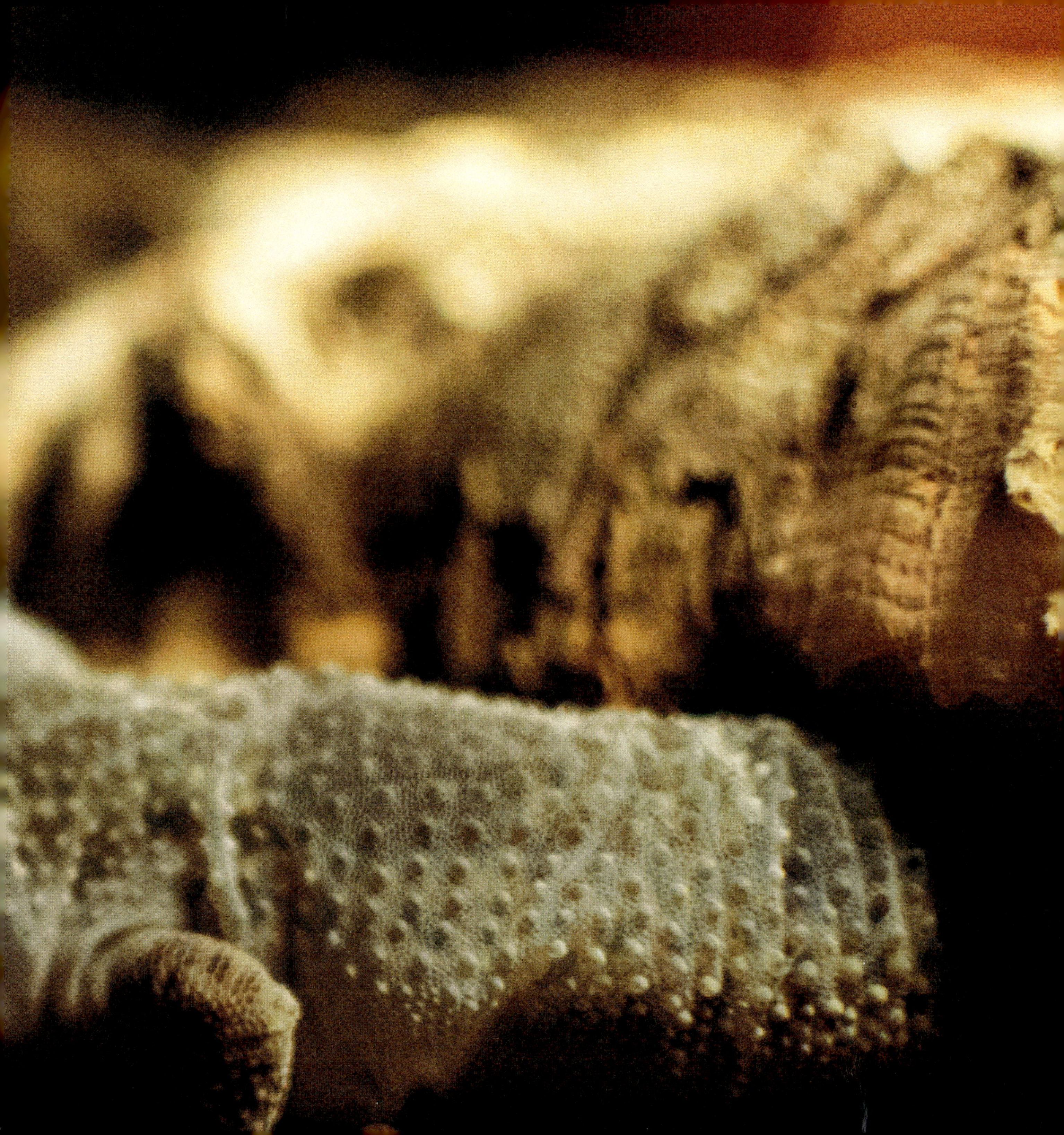

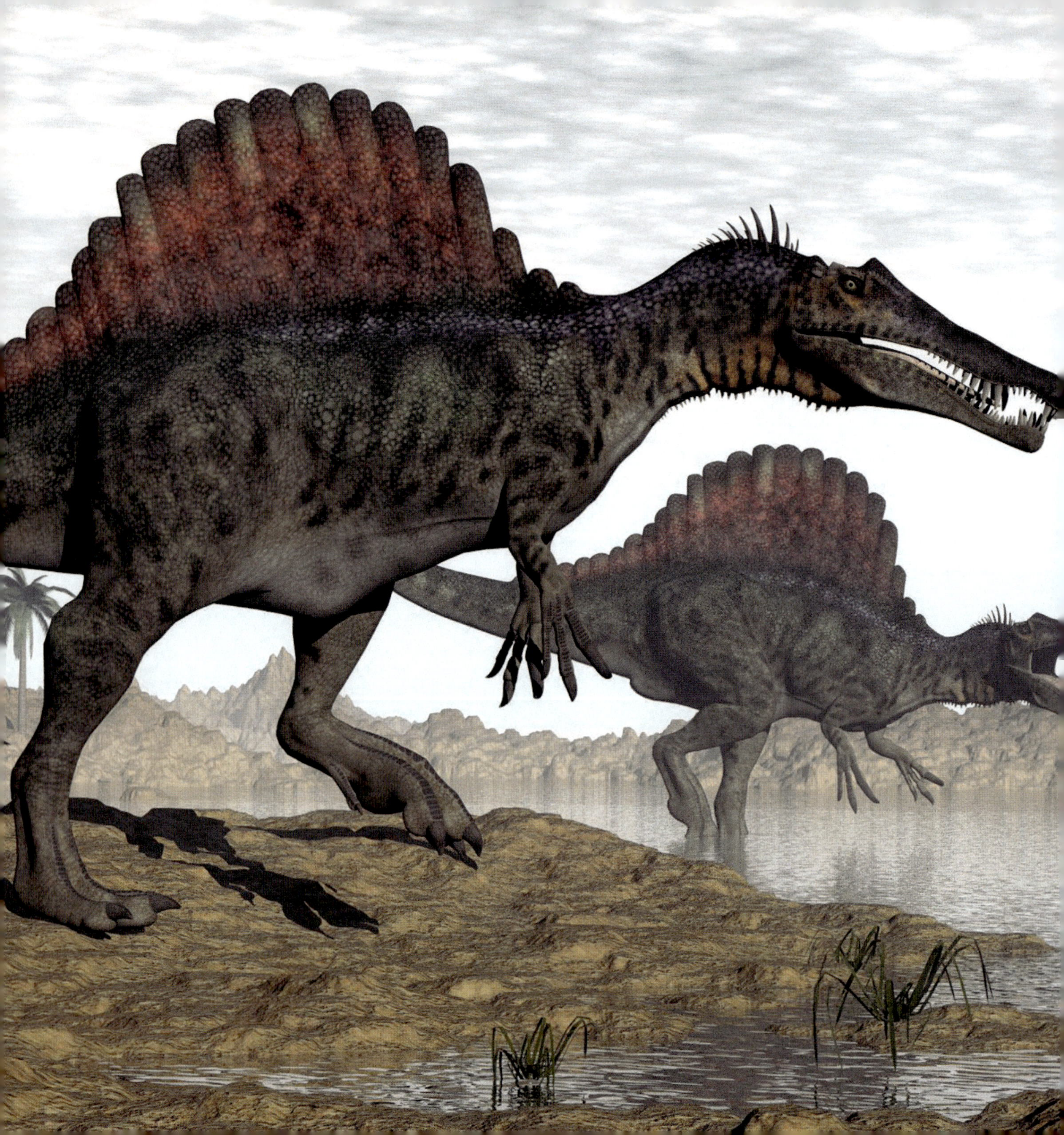

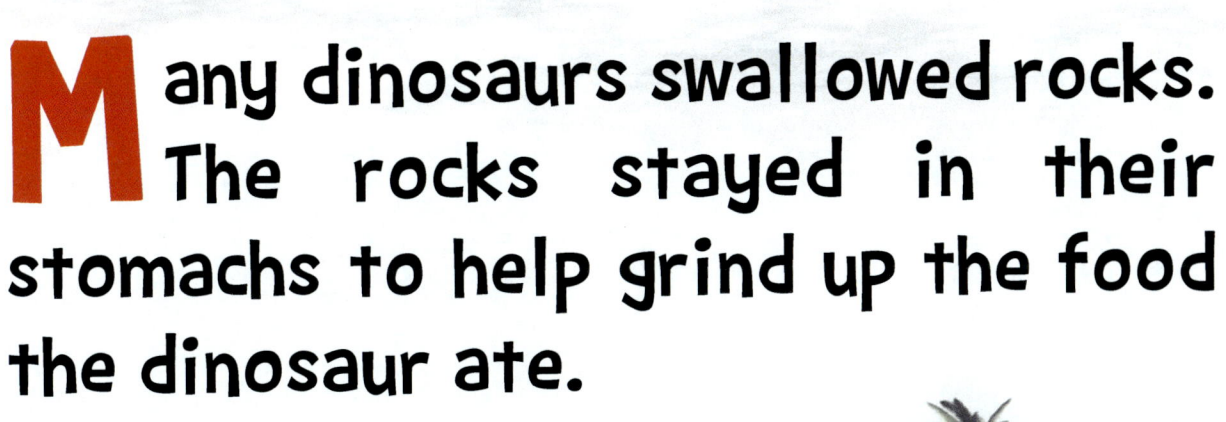

Many dinosaurs swallowed rocks. The rocks stayed in their stomachs to help grind up the food the dinosaur ate.

The sauropods were probably the tallest animals that have ever lived. Some would have been twice as tall as a modern giraffe.

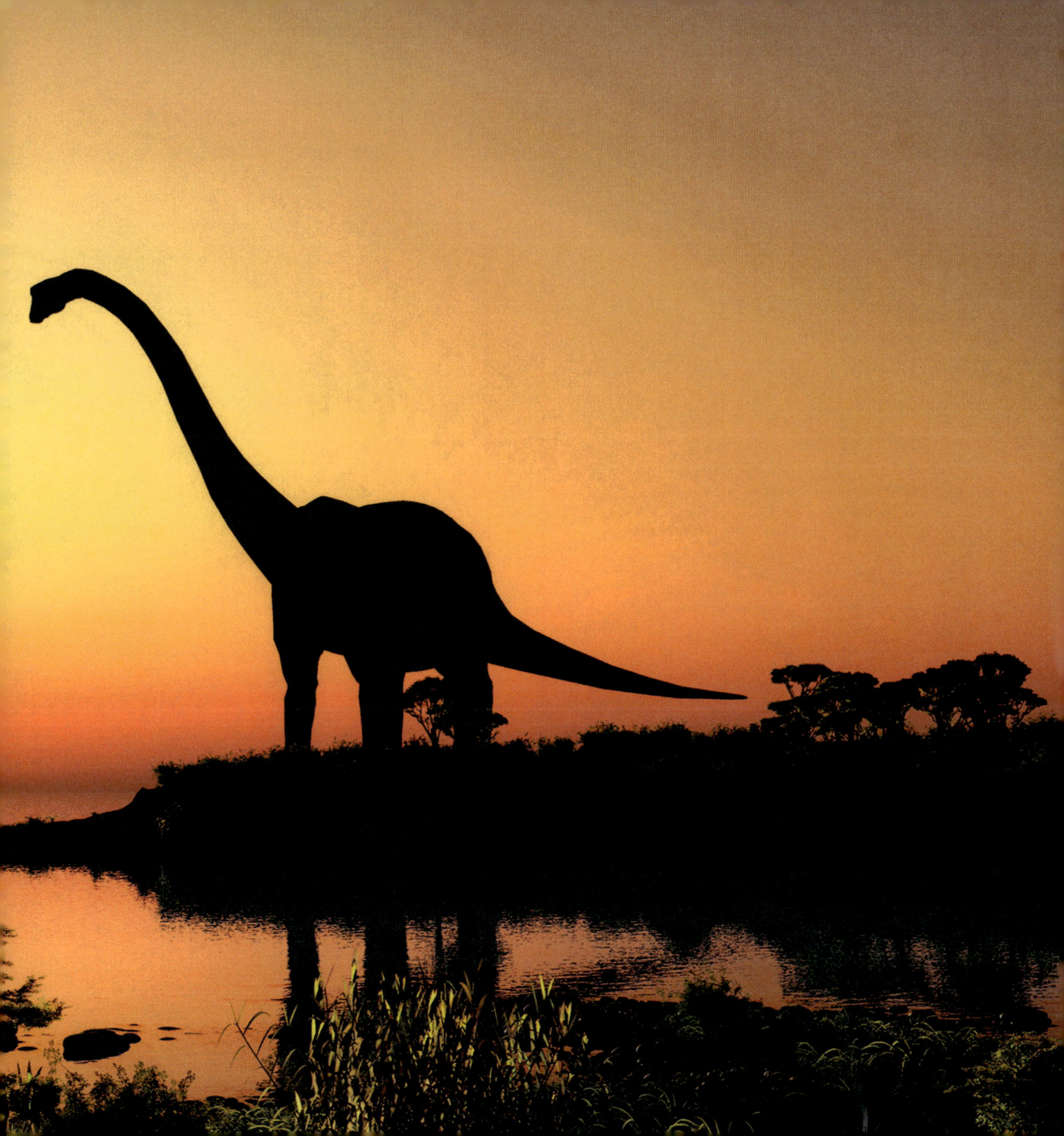

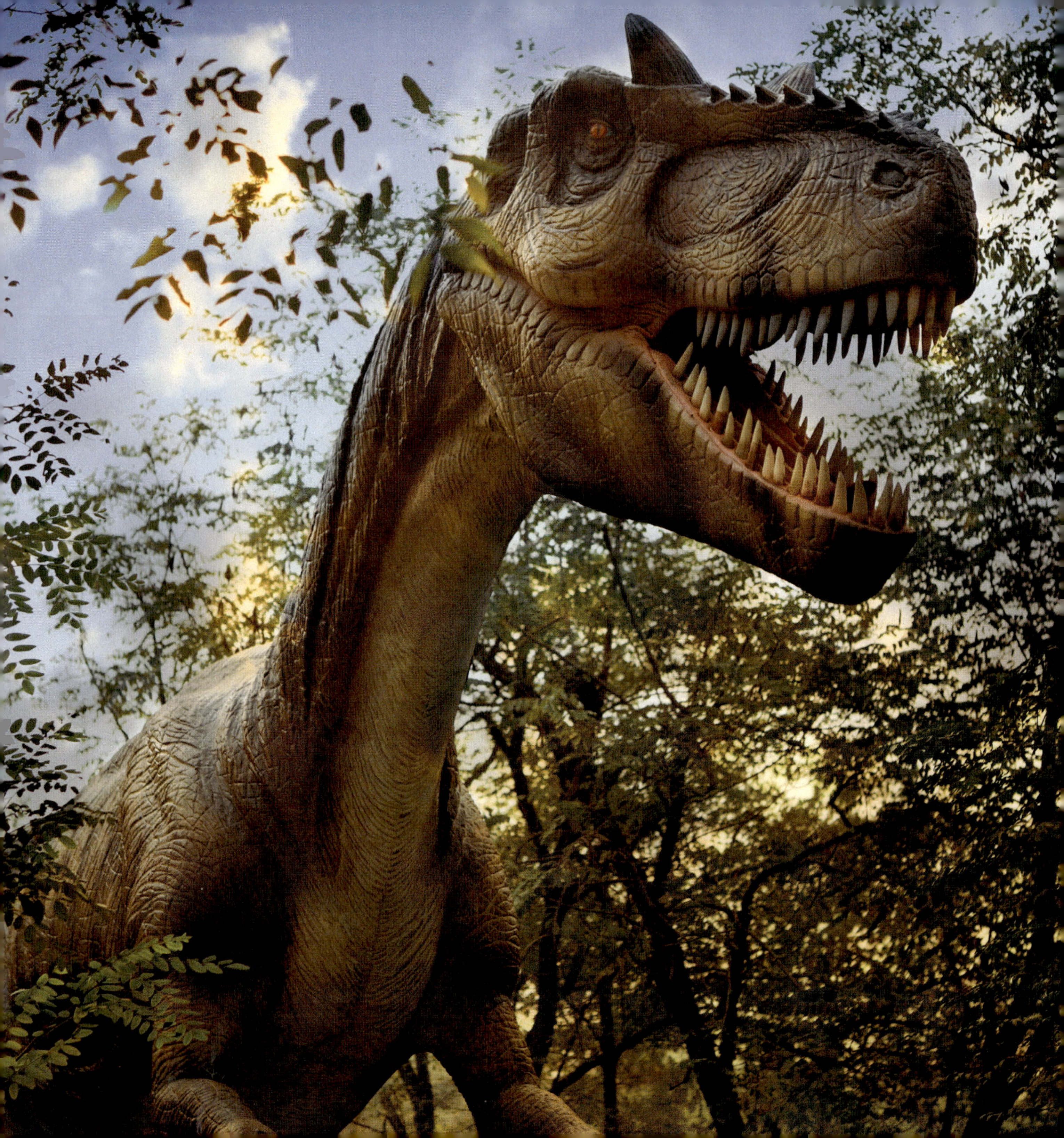

Meat-eating dinosaurs had sharp teeth and claws they could grasp and slash with. Plant-eating dinosaurs had more defensive weapons, like spikes or horns on their heads and bodies. Some had armor plating, the way modern turtles have shells that help defend them against attacks.

FINDING DINOSAURS

Most of the dinosaur remains we find are in sedimentary rock. This is rock that was mud, sand, and loose soil when the dinosaur died. Insects and small animals ate what they could of the dinosaur and left its bones and sometimes some of its skin behind.

The loose material slowly covered up the bones, and then, over thousands of years, compressed into rock. The bones we find have become fossilized—turned into rock themselves, but keeping the shape of the dinosaur's bones.

We have found dinosaur bones on every continent. The first great finds were in Mongolia and in the western United States. China and Argentina are home to recent, exciting finds.

THE END OF THE DINOSAURS?

Almost all the dinosaurs died very suddenly, about 65 million years ago. Scientists have some theories about how this happened, but nobody knows for sure.

One theory is that a meteorite about six miles across hit the earth. It may have hit what is now Mexico; scientists have found a crater there which is over a hundred miles across. Such a collision would have been a disaster for large land animals and flying creatures.

There would have been a shock wave flattening animals and forests, and a huge, global cloud of dust and debris that would have blocked light from the sun and poisoned the air. The effects would have gone on for many years, and any species larger than a large dog could not have survived.

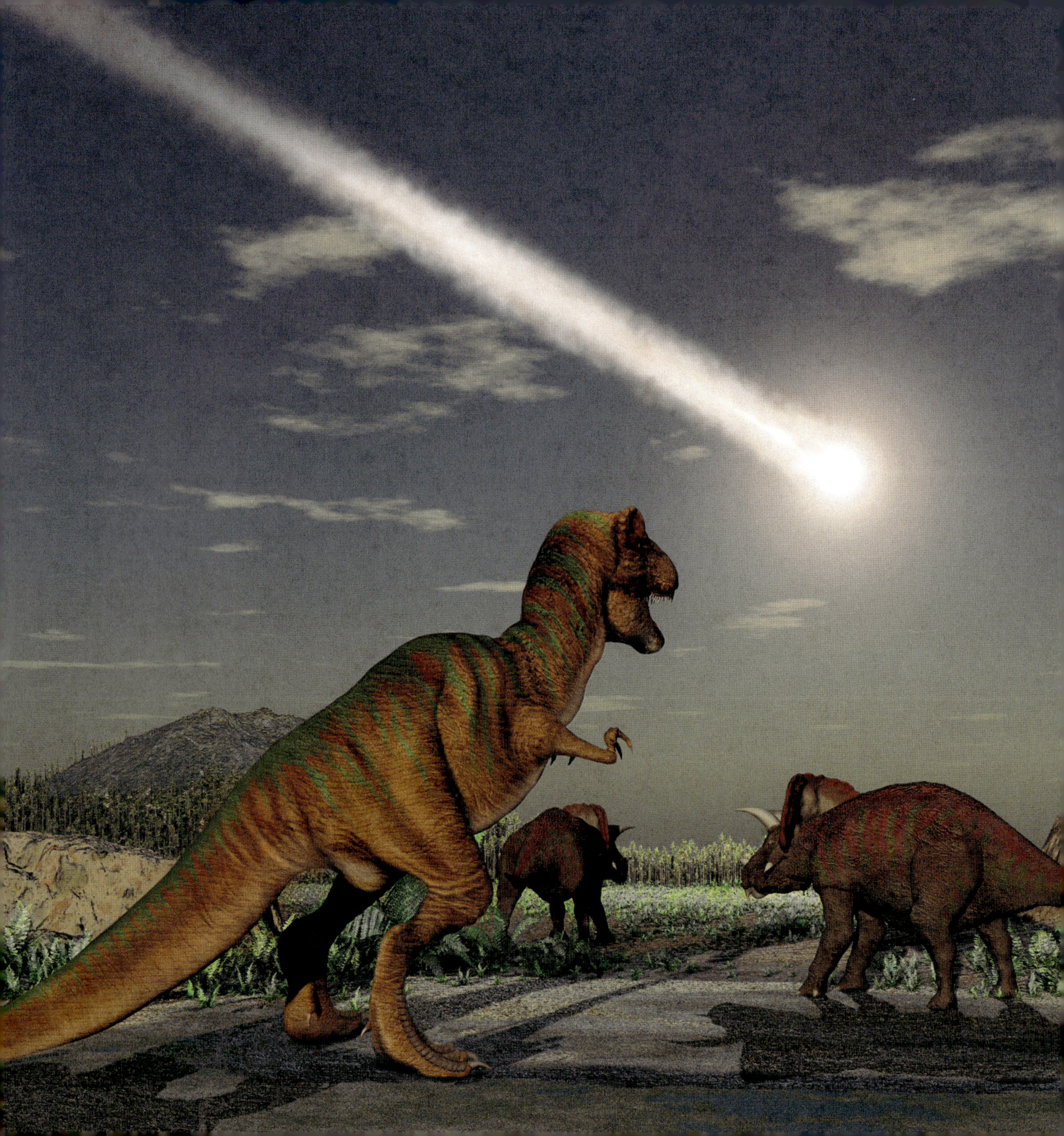

Some creatures survived this disaster, including sharks, alligators, jellyfish, insects, turtles, small lizards and birds, and crocodiles. Somewhere among the small creatures who made it through was the species from which humans eventually evolved. But all the dinosaurs, who had ruled the world for so many millions of years, were gone.

There are other theories about the dinosaur die-off that are less dramatic. One is that the expansion of small mammals (including our ancestor!) meant there were more mammals eating dinosaur eggs in the nests, and this cut down the reproduction rate until the dinosaurs died off. Climate change, not related to a meteor strike, could also have played a part.

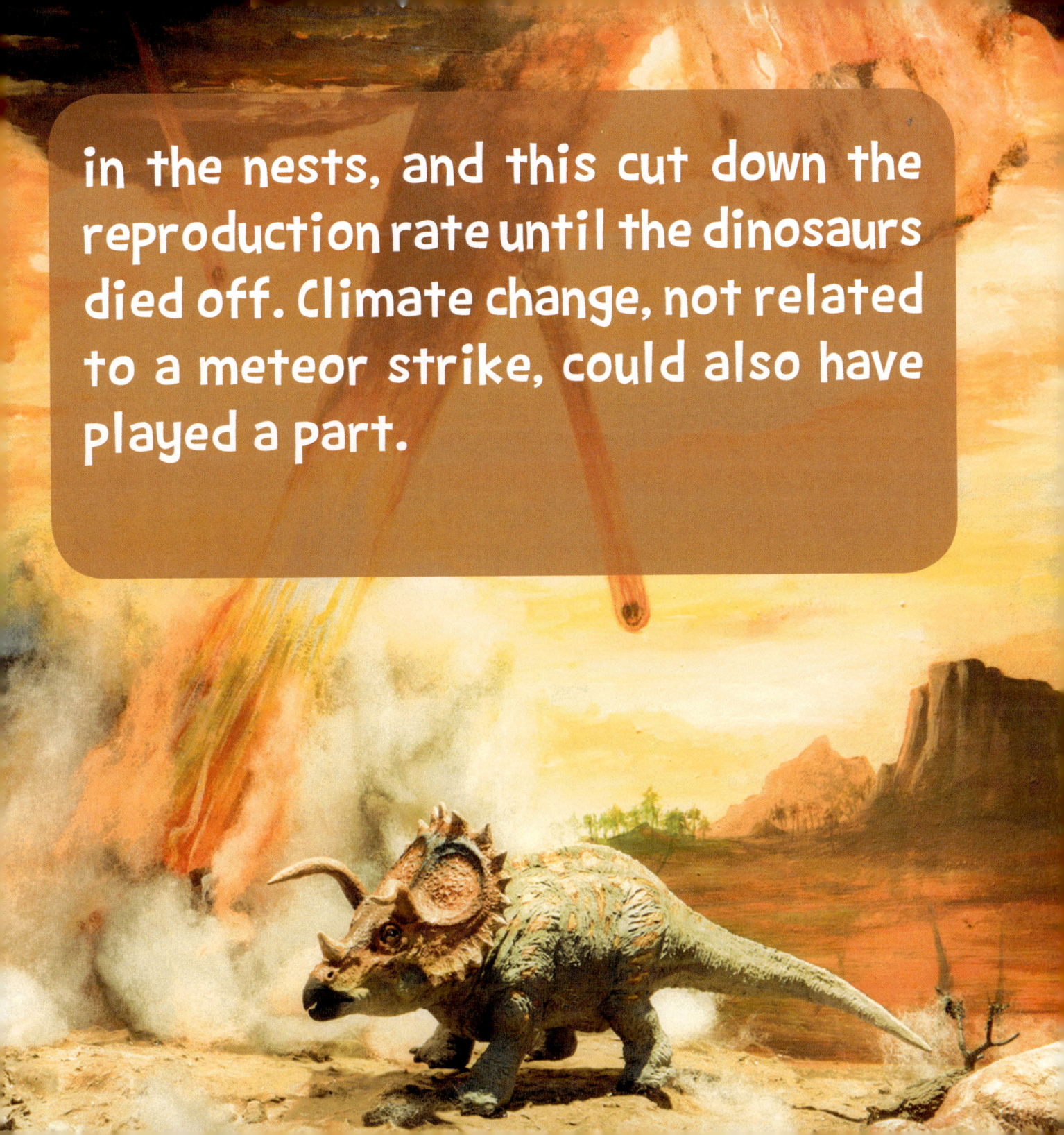

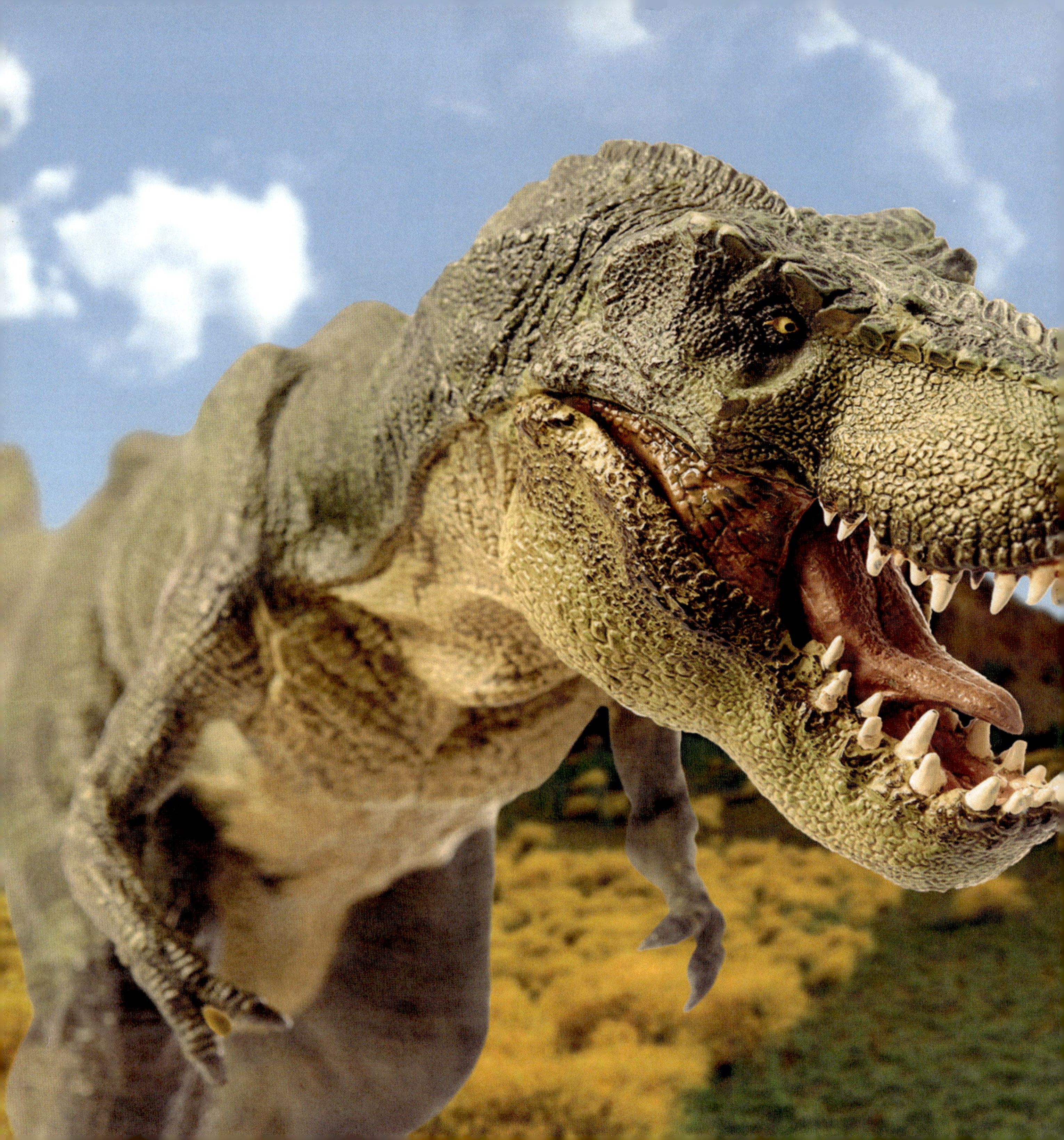

LEARN MORE

There is much more to learn about our world! Read more Baby Professor books to find out more about dinosaurs, the earth, animals and plants, and even human beings.

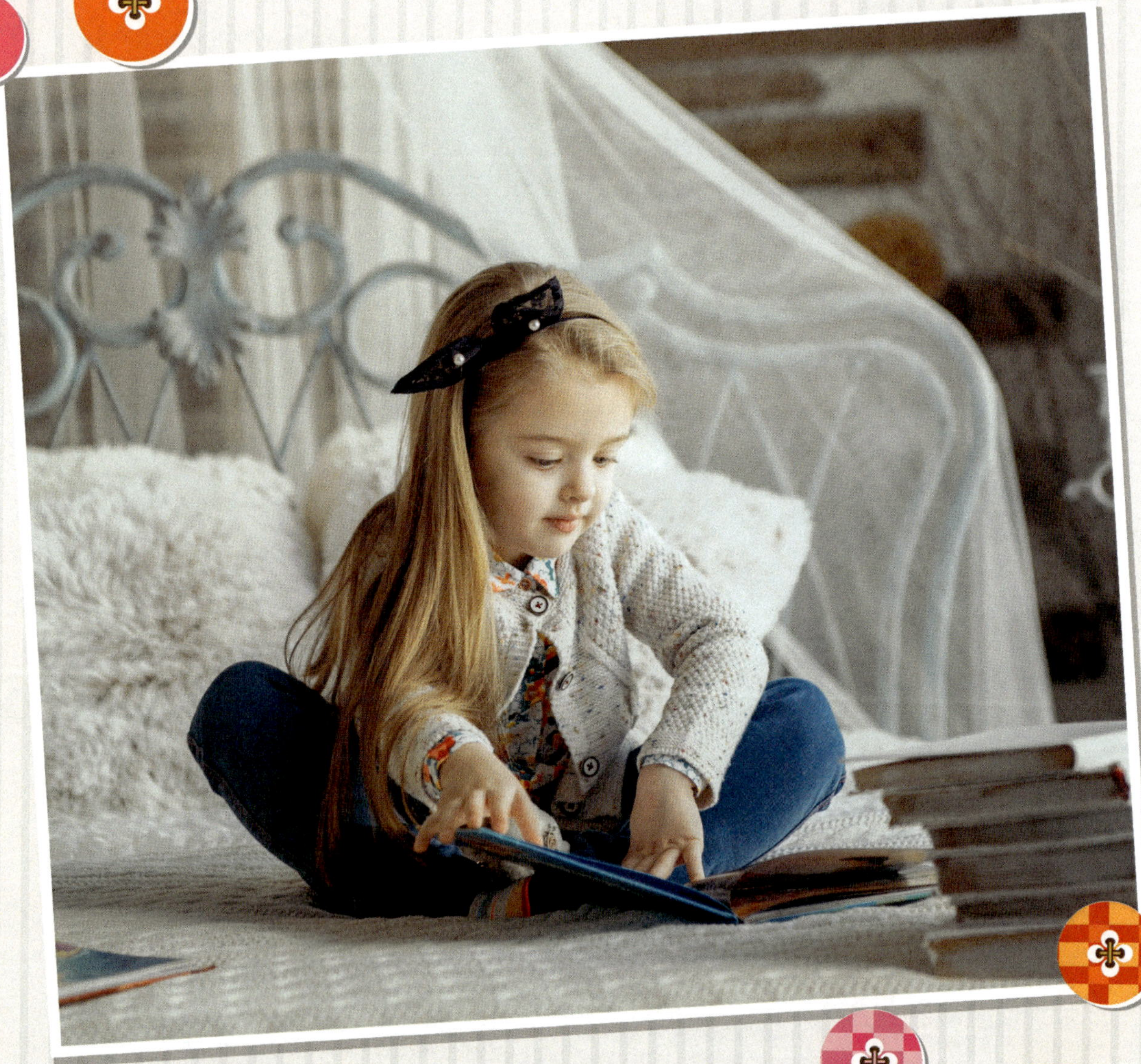

Visit

BABY PROFESSOR
EDUCATION KIDS

www.BabyProfessorBooks.com

to download Free Baby Professor eBooks
and view our catalog of new and exciting
Children's Books

Made in the USA
Middletown, DE
15 October 2020